www.MicroshareINTL.com/NewRules

www.MicroshareINTL.com/NewRules

7 NEW MARKETING RULES

A PROVEN SYSTEM FOR GROWING YOUR BUSINESS

BY BARRY SCHIMMEL & GRANT POLACHEK

www.Microshareintl.com

Copyright 2013 Barry Schimmel and Grant Polachek

All Rights Reserved. No part of this book may be reproduced in any form or by any means, electronic or mechanical, including photocopying, recording, or by any information storage and retrieval system, without permission in writing from the publisher.

Published by Microshare Intl LLC, S. Barrington, IL

Disclaimer: When addressing financial matters we've taken every effort to ensure we accurately represent our programs and their ability to improve your life or grow your business. However, there is no guarantee that you will get any results or earn any money using any of our ideas, tools, strategies or recommendations, and we do not purport any "get rich schemes". Nothing in this book is a promise or guarantee of earnings. Your level of success in attaining similar results is dependent upon a number of factors including your skill, knowledge, ability, dedication, business savvy, network, and financial situation, to name a few. Because these factors differ according to individuals, we cannot and do not guarantee your success, income level, or ability to earn revenue. You alone are responsible for your actions and results in life and business. Any forward-looking statements outlined in our book, or any other Microshare Intl materials, are simply our opinion and thus are not guarantees or promises for actual performance. It should be clear to you that by law we make no guarantees that you will achieve any results from our ideas or models presented, and we offer no professional legal, medical, psychological or financial advice. If legal advice or other expert assistance is required, the services of a competent professional should be sought.

www.MicroshareINTL.com/NewRules

SPECIAL OFFER

Microshare's $10K Marketing Strategy:

- Free One-On-One Consultation
- Spend 30-40 minutes working together to solve your business problems and create a plan for growing your business
- Everyone who applies for a consultation receives <u>9 complimentary bonuses</u>

4 WAYS TO REGISTER

Mobile Text
Text your name and email to 847-666-5670

Voice
Call 847-666-5670

Web
Visit www.Microshareintl.com/FreeConsulation

QR Code
Scan>>>

www.MicroshareINTL.com/NewRules

DEDICATION

This book is dedicated to...

My mom, Sue Hardman, and dad, Burt Schimmel, whose guidance throughout my life was everything that was needed. They taught me to work hard, be honest, and follow my dreams.

My wife of fifteen years, Jennifer, has always been an inspiration to me and to our two children, Alec & Elissa. She always gives us unconditional love and support.

My best friend and partner, Grant Polachek, whose vision and dedication made this book possible.

ACKNOWLEDGEMENTS

This book couldn't have happened without so many people that I need to thank. First and foremost is my wonderful family. My amazing wife, Jennifer, is the person who inspires me to accomplish so much. Alec and Elissa are my whole life and without them I wouldn't be the person I am.

My business partner Grant has given me the opportunity, time and help to get this book completed.

I am deeply grateful to everyone who stood by us and believed. I thank all in my personal and professional circles who influence me. I thank me editor, Kelly Epperson. I especially thank my clients who are using these 7 new rules of marketing to great success in their businesses.

www.MicroshareINTL.com/NewRules

www.MicroshareINTL.com/NewRules

TABLE OF CONTENTS

- Barry's Introduction 11
- Grant's Introduction 13
- Framework 15
- How to use this book 16
- Discovering The New Rules 19
- Rule #1: Develop a Strategy 23
- Strategy Case Study 42
- Rule #2: Start A Conversation 47
- Website Strategy Case Study 58
- Rule #3: Get Found 63
- Getting Found Case Study 72
- Rule #4: Build Authority 77
- Authority Case Study 86
- Rule #5: Market Your Reputation 89
- Reputation Marketing Case Study 99
- Rule #6: Automate your Follow Up 103
- Automate Your Follow-Up Case Study 113
- Rule #7: Target New Prospects 117
- Last Case Study: Microshare INTL 127
- Conclusion 133
- About The Author 134

www.MicroshareINTL.com/NewRules

BARRY'S INTRODUCTION

Is your business growing, struggling, or both?

Before we begin, let me tell you why I titled this book *7 New Marketing Rules*:

- **7:** You will discover a systematic seven step framework for success.
- **New:** The economy has changed, communication has changed, and we "the people" have changed; therefore, you cannot run your businesses, and your marketing campaigns, as if it were still the 90's.
- **Marketing:** These Rules are all about the activity of growing your business.
- **Rules:** I have tested, honed and proven this system. These Rules work.

The aim of this book is not to teach you the newest marketing strategies, but to provide you with a proven and repeatable method for success. It is my desire to convey a clear and simple step-by-step process for understanding and strategically implementing these New Marketing tactics, with the result of growing your business.

The underlying belief behind this book is:

The world is changing.

If you don't believe this simple axiom, if you want to run your business as if an extraordinary revolution is not taking place, then this book is not for you.

I am writing for the person who realizes that things are different, but who wants to succeed anyway.

My promise is that this current revolution is not a death sentence for your business. The savvy marketer who understands the demands being placed on current businesses can beat the odds and realize massive growth.

In the pages to come, I will teach you deep marketing rules. What I truly aim to do is facilitate your business's growth in our changing world.

www.MicroshareINTL.com/NewRules

GRANT'S INTRODUCTION

Marketing is an action...
...and practice makes perfect!

Therefore, the marketer must hypothesize, test, refine and repeat.

In the new world, the more methodical action you take, the more results you will get, and the more your business will grow.

You're probably familiar with the 4 P's (Price, Product, Promotion, and Place) and even the newest P (Positioning). You know the 4 C's (Consumer, Cost, Communication, and Convenience) and the other 4 C's (Commodity, Cost, Communication, and Channel). You've heard the newest buzzwords like: inbound, viral, purple-cow, and word-of-mouth; and likewise you recognize Social Media Marketing as a great way to grow your business. You also know that the most important Social Platform is Facebook, or maybe Twitter, or Four Square, or is it Pintrest or Google Plus... (I can't keep track).

If you are tired of the *hype-strategies of the moment* and countless gurus selling products that teach these strategies, then this book is for you. It will help you sort through the fog, clear away the clutter, and most importantly, develop a long term marketing plan.

The pragmatic marketing formula laid down in this book will easily integrate with your current marketing toolkit to make your campaigns faster, easier and more effective. With our system, you don't have to be a seasoned marketing expert to get real results (although it will benefit the marketing veteran too).

In the pages to come, you get the step-by-step guide to help grow your book of business.

FRAMEWORK

Through this systematic approach, you will build the business of your dreams.

HOW TO USE THIS BOOK

The first time you read this book, focus on understanding the big picture. Emphasize synthesizing each Rule completely, and visualize how the Rules work synergistically. Imagine how your business would benefit if each rule was followed.

Ask yourself, what would happen if my company:

- Developed an Effective Strategy?
- Controlled the Conversation with Prospects?
- Was Easy to Find?
- Commanded Authority?
- Was Known for its Outstanding Reputation?
- Automated Follow-up Effectively?
- Reached Targeted Prospects?

www.MicroshareINTL.com/NewRules

There is a second way to use the framework taught in this book.

When I coach clients, my primary goal is to pinpoint which Rule they are stuck on.

First, you must look at the framework as a step-by-step process. I start by analyzing their strategy, and then I look at their website. Next, I scrutinize their search results; I examine their authority, and so on.

My method is to stop when I find a gap. Once I've pinpointed their gap, I work with them to fix it. In this way, this framework is one of my most powerful tools for helping businesses grow. And through this book it can be yours as well.

There is one more important thing that I want you to know. Once you discover the gap—the problem—you can systematically work through the framework one Rule at a time, building a solid foundation.

Every time you work through all the Rules systematically, your marketing will be more consistent, more effective, and you will get better results.

If you want us to help you with this process, register for a free one-on-one consultation at www.Microshareintl.com

This framework is not a mere tactic, but a way of doing business. And for this reason you should continually return to this book, take notes, memorize the framework, and…

…print out the system steps, tape it to your desk, and measure, measure and measure your results along the way.

DISCOVERING THE NEW RULES

It's very important for you to realize that the first step to developing the New Rules was mastering the old ones.

Before opening my marketing company—Microshare Intl—in 2010, I had grown three multi-million dollar businesses. Prior to that, I received traditional training while earning my MBA from Roosevelt University in Chicago, IL.

While running my companies, I always knew that it was crucial to keep my finger on the pulse of my marketing. After 20 years, I've learned what works and what doesn't.

I connected with Grant to help me start Microshare—he was a founding member—and he brought a lot of marketing knowledge to the table. His experience was different from mine. It was in Grass Roots Marketing. For over ten years he had been helping to grow karate programs for National Karate (the largest martial arts organization in the Mid-West).

In the introduction, I joked about running your business like it is still the 90's. But in truth, this was a huge hurdle I personally had to overcome. I was very successful during that wonderful decade, and I had mastered the marketing techniques that got results. I truly wish that the methods that worked then still worked now. It would have saved me hundreds of thousands of dollars, because that is how much it cost me to learn the New Rules that are laid out in this book.

There were three important stages that I went through in discovering these Rules. First, as I already stated, I had to admit that there was a problem (sound familiar?). I realized that the world was changing and that the strategies that I had used to grow businesses before were not working anymore.

Next, I had to take action. The second and third steps I took simultaneously. I learned from the most effective and cutting edge marketers, and I executed countless campaigns.

This book is the culmination of myriad of books read; dozens of trainings, seminars, masterminds and coaching programs; and hundreds of failed campaigns.

In the following sections, I will teach you the Rules that have taken me many years and a lot of money to learn. You will come away with a framework, a systematic approach, which you can apply time and time again to get results.

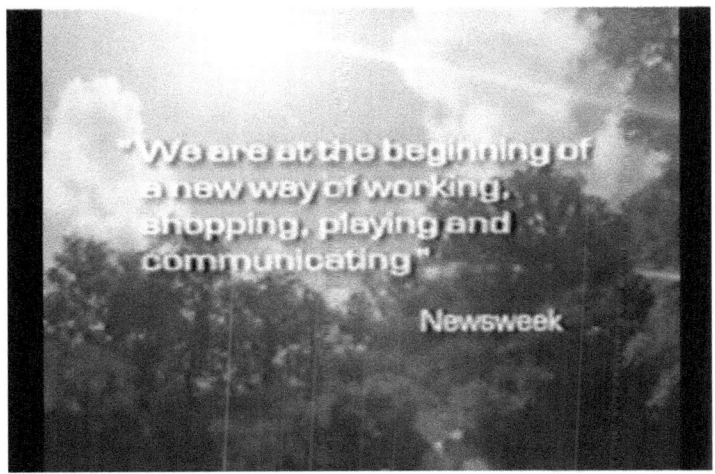

www.MicroshareINTL.com/NewRules

www.MicroshareINTL.com/NewRules

RULE #1: DEVELOP A STRATEGY

It is absolutely essential to have a Marketing Strategy for business growth.

Myth: Marketing is the same as Lead Generation.

Marketing genius Jay Abraham broke marketing into three parts:

1. Increase Leads
2. Increase Lead Conversion
3. Increase Existing Client Conversion

When working on your Marketing Strategy, Abraham's cycle should be approached in reverse. First work on your current clients, then on increasing conversions, and finally on increasing leads.

With this in mind, let's examine the 7 New Marketing Rules against Abraham's 3 parts of marketing, and then answer the question: What is the difference between Lead Generation and Marketing?

1. **Developing Your Strategy** has two essential parts: analyzing and

planning. You must analyze your fulfillment, conversions, and leads; evaluate your current strategy, engagement, presence, authority, reputation, automation and targeting; then plan growth across all of these areas.

2. **Starting a Conversation** is about converting more prospects and communicating with your current clients to increase repeat sales.
3. It may seem counterintuitive, but **Getting Found** is more about conversions than leads. The foundation of Getting Found is optimizing your online presence so prospects can find you when researching your company and your solutions. In this way, a robust online presence will have a larger effect on your conversion percentage than on the number of leads you generate.

4. **Building Authority** is about increasing conversions and developing a long-term relationship with clients. Having authority will build trust. Also, authority separates you from the competition. It is a powerful tool for cultivating brand loyalty.
5. **Marketing Your Reputation** has the same role as Building Authority: it increases conversions by promoting trust. Testimonials are second only to word-of-mouth referrals when it comes to getting prospects to trust you.
6. **Automating Your Follow Up** is another tool for increasing conversions. By automating your follow up, you will deliver your best presentation every time and follow up with more prospects, and more efficiently. In this way you will convert more leads to sales.

7. It is not until the last Rule, **Targeting New Prospects,** that you really focus on amassing more leads.

From this comparison, let me clearly explain the difference between lead generation and marketing.

Marketing is a systematic way of growing your business. In Abraham's Framework, marketing is divided into 3 parts and I explain how to execute using 7 Rules. In both cases, lead generation is only a fraction of the marketing discipline.

Lead Generation consists of many activities including: cold calls, social media, trade shows, networking events, and so much more; and lead generation is always the last phase of a systematic marketing approach. It is the business that reverses Lead Generation from the end of their system to the beginning that struggles and fails.

With this foundational understanding in place, you must evaluate where you are now and where you intend to be a year from now (or even 5 years from now).

The Truth about Strategy

Richard Branson, legendary entrepreneur, said, "Business opportunities are like buses, there's always another one coming." The sad truth is that most business owners are constantly chasing after the next bus, instead of staying on one bus long enough to reach their destination. This is becoming even more prevalent in our fast paced social media driven world.

Many people believe that going viral (getting likes, views, shares and other social recognition), even just for a moment, will be their ticket to business success. But smart small and medium sized businesses are not buying into the hype. They are holding tighter than ever to their business and marketing plans; and they are using more reliable and scalable new marketing tactics.

In our marketing firm, Microshare Intl, we have seen many companies grow substantially—in influence and revenue—because of new marketing, but we have also seen numerous companies fail. The difference between success and failure was always in approach.

Successful companies have Marketing Strategies that guide and influence their new marketing actives; unsuccessful companies don't. This is true in every industry.

So, what is a Marketing Strategy?

A Marketing Strategy is simply a written plan of how you are going to use marketing tactics to reach specific and relevant business goals.

Let's back up a little before we discuss this any further. According to Wikipedia, a business is "an organization involved in the trade of goods, services, or both to consumers" and marketing is "an organizational function" This means that marketing is an *activity* performed by your businesses to aid in the trade of goods and/or services.

Change the World and Make Money

In my experience, all businesses function for two reasons:

1. To fulfill a mission (think Mission Statement)
2. To generate revenues

Most companies try to accomplish both, but in in varying degrees. As a generalization, not-for-profit organizations lean towards trying to fulfill a Mission, where large publicly held corporations focus on revenues.

With this in mind, a Business Strategy is a systematic approach to optimizing business actives.

The gap between the current state of a business and the targets laid out in a business strategy create organizational needs. Examples of organization needs would be to reduce costs, increase productivity, generate more leads, or convert more leads.

As you can see from these examples, there is not difference between a business and marketing strategy. A Marketing Strategy is simply a subset of a Business Strategy.

Now, take a moment to think about some of your favorite brands.

Do Apple, Red Bull, and Cisco have different organizational needs compared to you?

Now shift your thoughts back to your own company. Your company is a machine built to generate revenue and change the world.

"Everything has a purpose, clocks tell you the time, trains take you places. I'd imagine the whole world was one big machine. Machines never come with any extra parts, you know."
– Hugo Cabret

This is where the real breakthrough of taking many ideas and activities and turning it into a precise Marketing Strategy takes place.

Metrics vs. Mission

Running a business is about making money and changing the world, delivering something of substantial value to your customers.

When it comes to developing a powerful marketing strategy there are certain metrics that you need to know:

- Average Transaction Value
- Average Lifetime Value
- Cost Per Lead (per campaign)
- Cost Per Sale (per campaign)
- Goal Income (Business & Personal)

But numbers aren't everything. One of my favorite business books, *Obliquity by* John Kay, reminded business owners to focus on their Mission.

Here are some great questions that I love to ask my clients, and sadly most of them don't have answer for them:

- What do you love about your business?
- What legacy do you want to leave?
- What have you done in the past toward that legacy?
- What is your company's Higher Purpose? (For example the online shoe store Zappos says, "We are all part of something great... To put a smile upon your face.")

Although it is not a hard statistic, your influence is a great indicator of future income. To track your influence monitor:

- Referrals
- Email Open Rates
- Social Engagement
- Video Views

Remember that all metrics are only indicators of success and in this way they are not perfect.

That is why you must balance your metrics with a core belief, a compelling Mission.

Only through this balance will your create a successful Marketing Strategy and a fulfilling business.

Marketing Decision

To create a Marketing Strategy, you must make marketing decisions based on your current organizational needs. Your decisions should be unique to the variables that are creating your current business atmosphere.

This means that your decision needs to be made based on the state of your business, your industry, the overall economy.

Without looking back to the basic core of your business, you will never create a successful Marketing Strategy.

In his book, *The Practice of Management*, Peter Drucker is famously quoted as saying:

"There is only one valid definition of business purpose: to create a customer... Therefore, any business enterprise has two—and only two—basic functions: marketing and innovation." This is certainly some of the best advice on building a sustainable company.

The problem now isn't who has the best product, but who has the best Marketing Strategy to market their product or services.

Companies big and small who have a marketing strategy grow 3 times faster than the ones that don't.

Brainstorming

The first step to a good Marketing Strategy is brainstorming, because your business does not exist in a vacuum.

Your business is a journey, and a Strategy is a roadmap.

The major objective of brainstorming is to place your X upon the map, otherwise known as choosing your destination.

Think of it like this - if you could only go on one vacation in the next ten to twenty years, where would you go?

Many entrepreneurs think that they know where they're going, but they have not truly painted a detailed picture of their success.

Brainstorming is about creating crystal clear and measureable objectives for your future marketing activities that perfectly align with your organizational needs.

The first step is to gather all of the peripheral information about your current business situation. Once you have all of your charts, graphs, stats, employee feedback, customer comments, you can ask:

1. What are your company objectives and what are you trying to achieve?
2. In what areas of your business is it important to improve your results?

www.MicroshareINTL.com/NewRules

3. What have you tried already to address these issues?
4. What are your Marketing Objectives?

Analyze

After you have decided where you want to go, you must create a plan and determine how you get there. To stick with the map analogy, you must define your route.

The mountains, valleys, rivers, etc., that will determine your route are your audience, your competition and your resources. If you understand those three things, you should be able to create an accurate strategy.

A huge marketing decision that many companies are making right now is…

…To Social Media or Not to Social Media

The answer is in your audience and your resources:

1. Do you have a statistical significant number of prospects using specific social media platforms?
2. Do you have the resources to create valuable social content and to create an online community and then convert them into long term clients?

Execution

The third step to creating a Marketing Strategy that will change your business is planning your execution.

Once you've done the grunt work of determining the organizational needs that you will address and how you are going to address them, you have to lay out the details.

The outcome of your Marketing Strategy is a detailed document outlining the execution of your plan.

Don't fool yourself…

....Without this document, you do not have a marketing plan.

Marketing Strategy Session

The key to completing a Marketing Strategy is scheduling it. The time that you dedicate to brainstorming, analyzing and creating an execution plan is your Marketing Strategy Session. A true Marketing Strategy Session is an intense and time consuming activity.

A Marketing Strategy Session can easily take 20 or more hours, and when you work with an experienced agency they may put 40-80 plus hours into completing your Marketing Strategy.

Therefore, we have put together 8 Power House Strategy Questions for you. You can answer them in less than 15 minutes and still completely change your business. (Next Page)

8 questions that will help you market and grow your business.

1. What business are you in?
2. Who is your best client?
3. Who should your target market be?
4. Where do your leads come from?
5. What is your X factor?
6. What is your unique story?
7. What is your irresistible offer?
8. What are your sales funnels? (Upsells, Down-sells, Cross-Sells, Residual)

Sign up at
www.MicroshareIntl.com/NewRules
for a video that will guide you
through these
8 Crucial Questions.

STRATEGY CASE STUDY

Ed, a business lawyer, was struggling to grow his law firm.

We worked one-on-one with him to answer the Eight Crucial Business Growth Questions.

During this time, Ed had a few "aha" moments.

<u>He realized:</u>

1. His business wasn't growing because he was having trouble communicating his value to prospects.
2. He was not conveying his unique story.
3. He was not targeting the prospects he could provide the most value to.

We started by helping Ed solidify his unique value proposition and communicating his unique story. He needed to own and convey what set him apart from all the other business lawyers.

In the end, Ed used his company history, individual experience, and some high profile cases (with great results) to convey how he develops and executes his solutions for his clients. Ed does provide consistent and superior results.

We then helped him reframe his initial meeting with prospects. The goal was to demonstrate significant value up front.

We built a framework to illustrate his services and an approach to engage prospects with Ed's irresistible offer.

Secondly, we coached him to gather resources that could immediately help his prospect. Ed began sending an email prior to his initial client meeting listing resources he had gathered that could benefit folks coming to him. Further, he began calling his initial client meetings Consultations.

Next we helped him with retargeting. Part of this process was setting up some measurable goals for prospecting. We asked Ed to offer his Free Consultation to 20 prospects in his target demographic (after introducing himself and developing an initial relationship). Most importantly, Ed was to spend the majority of his time talking to people who fit his target demographic.

THE RESULTS

Now for the real test…

Was our hypothesis correct?

Over the course of a month, Ed approached 20 prospects and 16 of them agreed to meet for a one-on-one consultation.

The end result was 9 new clients.

…SUCCESS!

www.MicroshareINTL.com/NewRules

www.MicroshareINTL.com/NewRules

RULE #2: START A CONVERSATION

Get your prospect's attention and let them experience what it would be like to be your best client. In this way, they will truly know, like and trust you.

"The keystone in building is the stone on which the foundation and all the construction rests. Remove the keystone, and the foundation is unstable." - Nick Nanton

Dynamic vs. Static

In the old world—when companies first began using the internet as a marketing tool—a great website was a reproduction of an excellent marketing brochure: appealing graphics, company information, strong copy, and a powerful call to action. These websites are Static, and while they were cutting edge ten years ago, they are completely outdated today.

On the other hand, Dynamic websites allow companies to seamlessly communicate with prospects, clients, and even search engines. Dynamic tools include blogs, videos, marketing automation software, social media integration, eCommerce, etc. Every company should strategically integrate these tools in their website.

New Website Paradigm

I trace the idea of using your website to *Starting a Conversation* back to the direct response copywriters who discovered that the longer the letter they wrote, the more conversions they received. The hall of fame writer Gary Bencivenga once wrote a 98 page sales letter.

The conversions did not come because people wanted to read every word of the extended copy, but because the long—and well organized—letters allowed the writer to have a conversation with their prospects.

These long letters would have many headlines, sub-headlines, bullet points, etc. And they would be very easy to navigate. The prospect could skim through, stop where they wanted, and in so doing develop interest, overcome their own objections, and ascertain all of the information needed to make the purchase.

For most businesses, Dynamic Websites have replaced the long sales letter.

To hook the prospect, you need a strong value proposition. This would be a short statement next to your logo which in a few words explains exactly what benefit you provide and why they should use you. For example: "We design simple and elegant user experiences that succeed on THE WEB."

Your content should be written like you are talking with your best client. They need to know what the benefits are to them. Next, they need to know what services you offer.

A Website is the Keystone of your Marketing

No matter how you originally connect with a prospect, almost every single one of them will end up looking at your website before they buy from you.

For this reason your website must be:
- Perfectly Branded and
- Able to move prospects through the sales cycle

Perfectly Branded

Your business website is often a prospect's first real impression of who you are and what you do. This *is* your brand, which helps prospects get to know, like and trust you. Remember from our Strategy chapter, the core of your company is the product or service that you provide. But, your brand is the personality behind your deliverable.

- What feelings do you want to elicit in your prospects and customers?
- What kind of people do you have working to deliver your products and services?

- Who is your leadership team, and what does their personal brand convey about your shared brand?
- What is your USP (Unique Selling Proposition)? How are you different from your competition?
- What is your Mission and what is your Higher Value?
- And most importantly, what kind of customers are you trying to attract?

In summary, your website must be clean and professional while conveying your company's unique personality.

In the article from Inc.com, "The New Rules of Branding Your Business Online," Christine Lagorio explains, "Mastering branding online takes a lot more than a cool logo and catchy slogan.

Experts play by a fresh new set of rules.

It's no longer enough to have a sleek website, social-media presence, and consistent brand aesthetic online. The new rules of branding your business on the web have a lot less to

www.MicroshareINTL.com/NewRules

do with presentation, and a lot more to do with interaction."

Move Prospects through the Sales Cycle

There is a trending in modern marketing that I cannot be happier with. As Marketing Automation, Data Mining and the like become more popular, marketing and sales teams seem to be working together more and more closely.

Whether you have traditional sales people or you're using inbound marketing strategies to generate leads, the most important questions to ask when developing a website are:

1. What features should my website have that will allow me to move prospects through the sales cycle?
2. How should I develop my website to increase my revenues by 10, 20… even 50%?

At this point you could return to Abraham's 3 Parts of Marketing or our 7 Rules. Ask yourself:

- How can my website bring in new clients?
- How can my website increase my earnings per sales (hint: up-sells, down sells, and cross sells)?
- How can my website increase the amount I sell to my current clients?
- How can my website help me get found?
- How can my website increase my authority?
- How can my website support my 5-star reputation?
- How can my website integrate with my marketing automation?
- How can my website help me reach top prospects?

All Roads Lead to…

www.MicroshareINTL.com/NewRules

When creating your website, assume that every prospect and every client will not only see it, but want to engage with your company on it.

Let me repeat this. Always assume that every person you cold-call or meet at a networking event, everyone who likes, follows, thumbs up, and pins your content, everyone who sees you at a seminar or signs up for your list will see your website.

Therefore your website, just like a good sales person, has two functions:

- To leave a great first impression
- And to move prospects through the sales cycle

Planning the development or upgrade of your website is something that should be addressed during your next Marketing Strategy Session.

But for now, we have put together a short checklist of features that are essential. (Next Page)

4 Website Must-Haves:

1. Branded video with irresistible offer (establishes credibility)
2. Lead capture (giving away something prospects want, builds authority)
3. Video testimonials from clients (credibility)
4. Current reviews (posted from current clients for credibility)

Sign up at
www.MicroshareIntl.com/NewRules
for a video that will guide you through these
4 Must-Haves.

WEBSITE STRATEGY CASE STUDY

A local printing company, we'll call them The Print Guy, was expanding their operation. They knew their business very well, but wanted us to consult with them on Marketing Strategy to ensure their marketing continued to be suitable for their quickly expanding business.

After their initial consultation, we continued working through the framework. It was time for a website that started a conversation with The Print Guy's best client.

We integrated the findings from our extensive strategic research with the "4 Website Must Haves"

We crafted a video script for the The Print Guy's CEO for the front page of their website. This video used copywriting best-practices to engage the viewer and persuade that prospect to use The Print Guy's services. The video also established credibility and introduced the brand.

www.MicroshareINTL.com/NewRules

We added value to the visiting prospects by creating an irresistible foot-in-the-door-offer and gave it away for free. In turn, the prospects supplied us with their name and email (lead capture). By delivering this valuable free offer, we positioned the printing company as an authority and elicited reciprocity. Most importantly, through this exchange of content for their email, our client now had permission to continue marketing to these prospects (list building).

Next, it is very important to give the prospect the experience of being "your customer through your current clients." Therefore, we videotaped customer testimonials and posted current reviews on the front page of their website (Credibility).

The Results

Now for the real test….

We trained the sales people and office staff at The Print Guy to direct prospects to the website and watch the videos and read all the 5-star reviews.

The outcome: Sales increased and the sales cycle was shortened.

...Success!

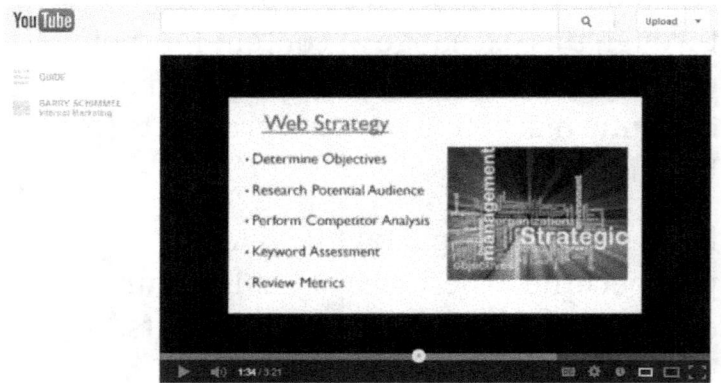

www.MicroshareINTL.com/NewRules

www.MicroshareINTL.com/NewRules

RULE #3: GET FOUND

By optimizing your Local Online Presence, you will put up your figurative "We're Open" sign online, simultaneously increasing conversions and generating leads.

www.MicroshareINTL.com/NewRules

To be a *real* word, the word must be in the dictionary. To be a *real* business, you have to be in…

… (This is where it gets tricky.)

In the old days, I could have confidently ended that sentence with "the Yellow Pages," but not anymore. Nobody really reads printed phone directories anymore. But these useful and important tools have not gone away. They have been replaced.

Instead of turning to the Yellow Pages to answer the age old question, "What's the d*@# number for the nearest plumber!?" People look online.

Getting Found is all about managing and optimizing your business on the new local landscape.

What makes this difficult for business owners is the vast number of Local Online Directories that exist. The major search engines all have them (Google, Bing, Yahoo, etc.). There are industry specific directories: Urban Spoon for restaurants, Angie's List for service contractors and Martindale for lawyers (just to name a few). Further, there are Chamber of Commerce directories; directories related to local news syndicates like Patch.com, even the Yellow Pages are making a strong run online with YellowPages.com.

The hard truth is that prospects are searching online to find you, but if you don't optimize your Local Online Presence, they may not find what you want them to.

Instead, they could find:

- Your competition
- Bad/negative reviews
- Blank directories that you have not claimed, making you look closed

When prospects go to a directory that does not have pictures, videos or reviews, it looks to them like that business is closed. Statistically, a prospect will never engage with businesses that have poor looking directories because it is a reflection of their brand.

With more than 60% of prospects searching the internet to find products and services, it is absolutely essential to do everything in your power to promote your business online.

Website Traffic vs. Getting Found

Before explaining this Rule any further, I want to make an important clarification. In new marketing, there are many ways to drive traffic, or get viewers to your website.

Here are some of the words that people use when talking about getting, or driving, web traffic:

- SEM Search Engine Marketing): is a broad term dealing with all ways of using search engines like Google, Bing and Yahoo to drive traffic. This is opposed to getting traffic directly from a Social Media site or a website.
- SEO (Search Engine Optimization): using your website and other content

like blogs, videos, PR, podcasts to get first page ranking on search engines like Google, Bing and Yahoo. When marketers are talking about Organic Search they are talking about SEO.
- PPC (Pay Per Click): is when you pay a search engine or any other website for each person who clicks on one of your ads.

But there are two distinct categories of people who will find you online:

1. People who already know about your company
2. People who know about your industry or solution, but don't know about your specific company

Rule 2, Getting Found, is about the former group (people who already know about your company). It is about making sure that these people can find you online. They need to find your website, find you on Google, Bing, Yahoo, and Yelp, and be able to find you and your employees on LinkedIn and Facebook, etc. And in this way, the purpose of Getting

Found is to support your Branding and your Authority.

On the other hand, Rule 7: Targeting Top Prospects, covers all aspects of driving targeted prospects to your website, known as lead generation.

From an execution standpoint, these two strategic business initiatives, Getting Found and Targeting Top Prospects through SEM, require very different tactics which will be explained later.

The Technology Revolution

This is a new frontier. The internet gives us information at our fingertips. Smart phones and tablets give us information at our fingertips everywhere we go.

We live in a fast paced society where our prospects have hundreds of ways that they can engage with our business - Different devices like computers, tablets, phones, or even in person. Different platforms like Social, Video, Review Sites, etc. It is in your best interest to be accessible.

Getting found is about being where your prospects are so they can find you, but not in an overwhelming way. You just need to give people enough information that they are willing to click over to your Marketing Keystone—your website.

Invite your Client to your Website

Here are some of the many places that your prospects may be looking for you online:

- Google
- Bing
- Yahoo
- Yelp
- FourSquare
- City Search
- Merchant Circle
- Yellow Pages

- Industry Directories (Urban Spoon, Avvo, Psychology Today)
- LinkedIn
- YouTube

Throughout the next four Rules, you will learn several more advanced ways of using the above tools for growing your business, but the first step is to simply show up.

Jeff Olson, the author of *The Slight Edge*, always says that the secret of success is "showing up, with a good attitude, over time."

Although there are many *tricks of the trade* that professional Local Search Engine Marketers use, you can succeed by understanding and implementing these three important steps in Local Search Marketing.

www.MicroshareINTL.com/NewRules

The 3 most important steps in Local Search Marketing:

1. Optimize the "big three" directories (Google Plus Business, Bing, Yahoo)
2. Analyze targeted directories and create business listings
3. Create and distribute video marketing campaigns

Sign up at
www.MicroshareIntl.com/NewRules
for a video that will guide you through these
3 Crucial Steps.

GETTING FOUND CASE STUDY

A popular local restaurant came to us because they did not know how to start using the internet to grow their business.

They were one of the oldest restaurants in a historic town. They had a great reputation and powerful brand loyalty. Because of this, we knew that they had a great X-factor along with an engaging story.

Furthermore, they had an effective website, but the gap was with their ability to Get Found online.

We started their Local Search Campaign by optimizing the big three directories:

- Google
- Bing
- Yahoo

(It is important to note that you must optimize these sites, not just claim them. Being on the best local directories does not mean you are at the top of them.)

Next, we evaluated, set up, and optimized dozens of other local directories. There are numerous important local directories, other than the big three that we optimized, including:

- Yelp
- Yellow Pages
- Four Square

We then strategically analyzed the restaurant niche to discover the most important directories for their specific industry.

Finally, we created a video marketing campaign and distributed it to hundreds of social sites to increase their online presence and boost their search engine rankings. We also loaded these videos to many of their local directories.

The Results

And how did this work for them?

This local restaurant ended up with a powerful local online presence, 1st page Search Engine Ranking, over 15,000 views each month from Google alone. Prospects are finding them before the competition. And they are now ready to make online reservations and book parties in their banquet room.

Success!!!

Today they are thriving.

www.MicroshareINTL.com/NewRules

www.MicroshareINTL.com/NewRules

RULE #4: BUILD AUTHORITY

The simple truth is people listen to people with Authority. People buy from those they Know, Like, and Trust.

A Great Anecdote

"My problem isn't that people don't love my product, it's that people just like their money more. I walk up to prospects every day and say to them, 'Do you want this, and this, and this benefit?' And they respond, 'Oh, yes!'

I say, 'Well, I have the perfect solution for you. Let me show you what I can do…' And they respond, 'Oh, fantastic! Great!' Then I say, 'Excellent. I'll give you all the benefits I just mentioned by selling you the solution that I just described.' And they respond, 'Oh, yes. That sounds outstanding!' And I say, 'All you have to do is give me this small amount of money.' And they respond, 'Oh, no…'"

A good friend of mine told me this story in jest. He has a flourishing business, but I think it touches upon a common marketing problem.

More Than a Great Product

In the ideal world, bringing a great product to the market would be enough. But in the real world, it isn't that simple; in the real world, you have to convince people to buy your great product.

There are many old school methods of persuasion that still work today, but since these are the New Rules, I will refer you to some classic books to learn these Old Rules:

- Joe Sugarman's *Triggers*
- Robert Cialdini's *Influence*
- Eugene Schwartz *Breakthrough Advertising*
- Robert Collier *Robert Collier's Letter Book*

With that said, in the new world, authority is the number one requisite for getting prospects to make a purchase and therefore, Building Authority is our Fourth Rule.

Building Authority with Content

Building Authority will help you earn trust...

...It is not trying to sell something, but giving away high quality content that will build your prospects confidence in you, your company.

Prospects are looking for real solutions. Once you have Authority, prospects will be confident in your ability and want to do business with you.

Sonia Simone, author of, "The 5 Cornerstone Values that Build an Authoritative Online Presence," states, "It's the authoritative site that earns the business."

It is important to follow the influencers in your industry, but it is more important to develop your own unique ideas and approaches.

One of the best ways to start building authority is by developing a visual framework around the core value of your solutions.

For example, this book is part of our Authority Strategy, and as you know, it explains a framework that can help you grow your business in the new economy.

The 7 Habits of Highly Effective People is based on a Visual Framework, and Neilson Marketing uses a framework to depict their integrated suite of solutions.

However you decide to structure building authority, prospects are always looking for great content from someone who doesn't have their own self interests in mind. And that is why content marketing works. It is a foot in the door strategy that will result in many loyal followers and raving fans.

Two high powered methods for building authority through content are:

1. Creating automated webinars that educate
2. Publishing books that help people solve problems

Seth Godin is a great example of someone who built their brand around authority. His

Authority Blogging is probably the best around today. He earned a tremendous amount of authority by showing up day after day for years, delivering something remarkable — concise, well-written expressions of his ideas.

Third Party Validation

Third party validation and borrowed credibility are two other very important concepts when it comes to Building Authority.

Third party validation is when you get someone else who already has authority to reinforce your messages. Third party validity could be a celebrity endorsement or being featured in the local newspaper.

The reason we utilize Press Releases to build Authority is because they provide instantaneous Third Party Validation.

Authority and Sharing

One of the great things about New Marketing is the ease at which content can be found and shared.

We love to use Press Releases because of the third party validation, but another important perk is that current news can be ranked in search engines within minutes of being released and many people who are searching can find the information that can solve their problem.

Press Releases will also build backlinks to your website. Then the Press Release can be tweeted, re-tweeted, liked on Facebook, Plus One'd on Google, etc.

The ultimate goal is to have a consistent brand that prospects get to know and trust. The more high quality content you create, the more people will engage with you.

Authority and Altruism

Building Authority is not only necessary for growing your business, but it gives you wonderful feeling knowing you made a difference in the world! This is one of the hidden joys of being part of a great business, knowing that you have contributed to something bigger than yourself.

Six Ways to Build Authority:

1. Distribute Press Releases
2. Develop Authority Blogs
3. Publish Books
4. Promote Webinars (Live and Automated)
5. Host Seminars
6. Get Engaged with Your Followers, Fans, and Subscribers (Facebook, LinkedIn, Twitter, YouTube & Forums)

Sign up at
www.MicroshareIntl.com/NewRules
for a video that will guide you through choosing the best way for your business to Build Authority.

AUTHORITY CASE STUDY

Susan, who has a Human Resource Consulting/Coaching Company, came to us because she was struggling with growing her business and reaching new prospects.

We started with developing a strategy, rebranded her web-site, optimized search results and now it was time to start building authority.

(It is important to build authority to help you earn trust in your industry. Authority is the number one requisite for getting prospects to trust you.)

Next, we researched where Susan's top prospects where hanging out online and what types of conversation they were having.

We then strategically analyzed the Human Resource niche to discover the most visited forums of their top prospects.

Finally, we created Press Releases and distributed to hundreds of social sites to increase Susan's company's online presence and boost her website's search engine rankings. She started blogging and became a guest blogger on popular sites. Additionally, Susan wrote and published a book.

The Results

Companies started contacting Susan to come speak at their functions. These were paid speaking engagements and as the subject matter expert (authority) presenting, she expanded her coaching and consulting business to her new audience. Referrals started pouring in and Susan was able to provide considerable value to prospects with all the great content she produced.

The end result was new clients...more money!

...Success!

www.MicroshareINTL.com/NewRules

RULE #5: MARKET YOUR REPUTATION

Would you buy a product or service that has bad ratings and reviews?

Two products are identical: The first one has 10 good reviews; the second one has 3 reviews & one of those reviews is bad. Which one would you buy?

Clients who improve their online reputation will increase sales. This is due to the fact that people are looking at your products/services and are reading the online reviews before they buy.

No matter what you are selling, reviews and testimonials are crucial. In the old world, the big publishers where able to greatly influence sales through their reviews: think Siskel and Ebert, Consumer Reports etc.

As in all new marketing, the power is now in the hands of the individual: think about the last time you bought something from Amazon or chose a movie on Netflix. I bet you stayed away from movies and products with 1 or 2 stars.

We are more and more digital. Online reviews now play a significant role in the perception of organizations as well as their products and services.

The sad truth is that no marketing techniques will work unless you first have a great reputation. Without at least six to ten 5-Star Reviews, businesses are viewed as being potentially untrustworthy. Therefore it is essential to position your company as the market leader with a five star reputation online.

Reputation on its own

In the introduction I asked you to pay close attention to how these 7 Rules work together synergistically. Reputation Marketing is the Rule that demonstrates synergy the most.

Before we get into synergy, let me explain a little bit about what reputation marketing is…

Reputation Marketing helps businesses improve their online reputation.

The key distinction between Reputation Marketing and Reputation Management is that Reputation Marketing is an action and Reputation Management is a re-action. Reputation Marketing is about actively building your reputation and promoting it.

The Reputation Marketing Process is:

- Create a System
- Build a Reputation Culture
- Promote Your Reputation

The key ingredient to your Reputation Marketing is testimonials and online reviews. So, a Reputation Marketing System allows you to efficiently collect and organize client reviews.

Promoting your Reputation means that you use these reviews in your marketing collateral: Brochures, Website, Local Marketing, Direct Marketing, etc.

Reputation Culture

Building a Reputation Culture in your business is a key component to successfully marketing your reputation.

A Reputation Culture is about training and motivating your team to use the system. Without a Reputation Culture, your Reputation Marketing will be dead in the water. If your team is not actively collecting 5-star reviews, then there will be nothing to promote to your prospects.

Reputation and Authority

Testimonials are a form of third party validation. Therefore, Reputation Marketing and Building Authority are twin Rules—they are inseparable.

Authority is your ability to get prospects to know, like and trust you. Testimonials are second only to word of mouth recommendations when it comes to trust. This is why your company's reputation is a key factor in why people choose to use you or to go with your competition.

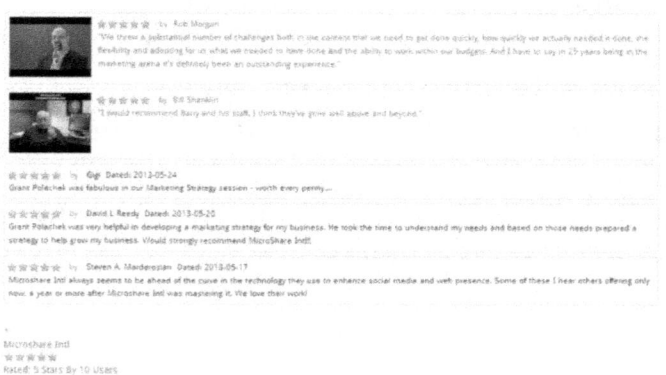

Reputation and Your Conversation

If you could have only two features on your website, what would they be?

Modern marketing genius Mike Koenigs teaches testimonials and a call to action are essential. Marie Forleo validated this by launching a high end coaching retreat—with a price tag of over $10,000—using a website that had nothing but testimonials and an add to cart button.

In particular, Video testimonials have a very powerful impact on prospects allowing them to experience what it is like to work with you before they ever buy. Therefore, adding video testimonials to the front page of your website is one of the quickest and simplest ways to increase your conversions and grow your business.

Reputation and Getting Found

Reputation Marketing and Getting Found are synergetic because they share the same platforms. Local Directories are the foundation of your company's ability to get found and local directories are the most prevalent place that customers level their online reviews.

The more reviews you have on each online platform, the more likely you will get found, and the more likely someone will click from the external directory to your websites. This is important because your website is built to move people along in the sales cycle and get them to call you.

Reputation and Targeting

Businesses need a Reputation Marketing System more than ever, because search engines like Google are scoring online reviews in search algorithms making it easy for prospects to choose the more reputable company.

Ten years ago, when the internet was very young, web developers used On-Site SEO to achieve top ranking on search engines. This means that they structured the content on their static website to get first page search engine rankings.

For several years now, the best way to execute effective Organic Search Marketing (SEO) was to use content—blogs, press releases, articles, podcasts, videos, social posts—in conjunction with a back linking strategy. This method is still used today and is necessary and effective. Google has more value on third party content like reviews and review sites.

Sites that feature reviews—Amazon and Local Directories—are powerful and respected by Google therefore giving your site authority when you are mentioned.

Search for you and your company and see what people are saying - or not saying - about you and your company.

Three Essential Facts

1. Consumers look up an average of 10 reviews before making a decision.

2. 70% of consumers trust a business with a minimum of six to ten 5-star reviews.

3. Google ranks your online reputation.

Sign up at
www.MicroshareIntl.com/NewRules
for a video that will guide you through the best ways for your business to Build Authority and Reputation.

REPUTATION MARKETING CASE STUDY

I was personally looking for a window washing company to come out and clean the windows at my house. I searched online and seven companies showed up on the first page of Google.

The first company listing had a 29/30 score (Extraordinary to Perfection), the second 9/30 (Poor to Fair), and the others had a few reviews but nothing to get my attention.

The company with a poor reputation was local and family owned. I believe in supporting the community and local businesses, so I decided to contact them. I was hopeful they could explain their 9/30 ranking and tell me why I should use them.

On to the Case Study:

When I called, the owner, Johnny, got right on the phone with me. He went on to explain his compelling company story and new customer specials (irresistible offers).

Johnny was troubled by my story of how I found him and what impact the negative reviews could have on prospects. After our open conversation, we were both sold.

I hired him, he hired me.

We setup a private testimonial page on his website where we could direct all of Johnny's happy customers to post reviews.

After the 5-star reviews were posted to his website, they were aggregated to review sites like Yelp, City Search, Merchant circle, etc. On the flipside, all negative reviews from his testimonials page were handled differently. We taught him how to contact anyone who left a negative review and work with them to remedy their poor experience. The influx of positive reviews diluted the few unhappy customers, and Johnny's company's 9/30 reputation score greatly increased.

Finally, we videotaped two customers who had given him a five-star review and posted the videos to the front page of his website with three more current testimonials underneath.

Prospects could now experience the benefit of using Johnny's company before hiring him, through the 5-star video testimonials of extremely satisfied customers.

In addition, we blasted these video testimonials to hundreds of social sites to increase Johnny's web presence and generate leads. At the same time, his 5-Star Reputation was posted on LinkedIn and Facebook.

The Results

Sales increased. Johnny's new reputation funneled prequalified, presold customers from the internet, away from his competition, into his sale cycle, because buyers trusted his reviews.

The end result is that his phone rang off the hook!

Success!

www.MicroshareINTL.com/NewRules

RULE #6: AUTOMATE YOUR FOLLOW UP

You would be rich if everyone who meets you for the first time buys from you.

Sales Rule: People buy from companies that follow up…

Relying on old methods like cold calling, direct mail pieces or belonging to a networking lead sharing group are no longer *enough* to attract Top Prospects. To be consistently effective, it is essential that you have a systematic approach with at least seven touch points.

The Old Paradigm

In Rule 2, I told you that a great website should function like a long sales letter, answering all of your prospects questions, overcoming all of their objections, and giving them all the information that they need to feel comfortable making a purchase from you. I also shared that one of the most powerful tools to put on your website was a lead capture tool. Let me tie this in with Rule 4, Build Authority, and then we will move on to Automating Your Follow Up.

www.MicroshareINTL.com/NewRules

If you are Building Authority, you should have great content that you are giving away for free: Books, eBooks, Automated Webinars, etc. So, what you do is give away some of this free content in exchange for your prospects email information. Once you have this, then you can send out automated emails with great content that provides value to your prospects, and at the same time brings them closer to purchasing from you. This is called a horizontal sales letter, because you are delivering the same great content that would be in a long sales letter, but you are doing it over time through automated, or drip, emails.

The New Paradigm: Cross Channel Marketing Automation

Wouldn't it be great if you were able to follow-up and get business from everyone that visited your website or that you met at a networking event or tradeshow?

What are you doing with all the business cards you have collected?

Would your business be impacted if you were giving your best presentation to each and every prospect you met either in person or they visited your website?

This Rule, Automating Your Follow Up, puts your online marketing concept on steroids.

If you're running even a nearly-decent company, you have at least three burning lessons, principles, or facts that you wish you could teach to every single prospect and client that you have. But the truth is that you just don't have time to sit with people one-on-one and educate them.

Are you tired of saying the same thing over and over and over again? Are you sick of working so darn hard to build relationships?

Introducing Marketing Automation!

Cross Channel Marketing Automation allows you to take your horizontal sales letter offline and bring it to networking events, tradeshows, speaking engagements, and business meetings.

It allows you to record your absolute best presentations and deliver them to your target while you sleep. And even more importantly, it allows you to deliver your messages in whatever way your prospects respond best (Email, Text, Voice... Audio, Video). If you can conceive it, then it can be automated.

Imagine someone watching your video on a smart TV while lying on the couch. Traditionally, you would end with a call to action that invites them to your website. But, what if they could simply take out their cell phone and text in to receive your valuable and informative content?

Or imagine that you are coming home from a tradeshow with dozens of business cards. What if you could use a mobile app to scan these business cards straight into your database—with permission of course—and automatically (or as a client of mine says 'like magic') send an informative PDF and video business card which contains video testimonials right to their inbox?

Value, Value, Value, Sell

If this seems complicated, let me simplify it for you.

Using technology, you can save time and make more money.

Here's the core concept behind Marketing Automation. When you sell, you cannot follow up with everyone the required seven times that it takes to close the average sale. So you are using your discretion to decide who to engage with. The problem is that even the absolute best salespeople are wrong a good percentage of the time. But with marketing automation, I close many clients who are not in A-List and even clients who I haven't spoken to in months. And these people definitely would have slipped through the crack if I didn't Automate my Follow Up.

Here's how it works…

When I meet someone, I put them in my database; when people go onto my website, I encourage them to sign into my database; when I engage on social media I encourage people to sign into my database. In this way everyone who expresses a genuine interest in my solutions gets funneled into my database.

But here's the secret, I don't sell them anything. Right away, I deliver value first to my prospects. I send them Case Studies, eBooks, Emails that educate, Press Releases, Videos, etc.

I give them something of great value before I ever ask them to buy something from me. I show them Results in Advance.

The trick is that all of this takes only 3 seconds of my time. Once I've set up my automated follow-up, all I have to do is enter prospects into my system—with their permission of course.

Warning

Now remember that Automated Follow Up is only a conversion tool. If you have a hot prospect who is ready to move forward, simply schedule an appointment and close them.

The point of automating your follow up is to increase your conversions by 50%, or even more. It will never replace the process of one- on-one selling but it does make it a lot easier.

Getting Started

There are many Automated Marketing tools and strategies. I recommend that you schedule appropriate time to plan your Automated Marketing in your Marketing Strategy Session (see Rule 1), or consult with a Cross Channel Marketing Expert.

Here is a list of 10 Marketing Methods. Make sure that the tools you choose are effective for the strategy you chose to go to market. Also, know how your prospects like to communicate.

(See the **10 Vital Cross Channel Marketing Methods** on the next page).

**10 Vital
Cross Channel Marketing Methods.**

1. Text Messaging
2. Email Auto Responders
3. Web Forms
4. Mobile Kiosk
5. Business Card Scanning
6. Voicemail Marketing
7. Data Mining
8. Social Profile Gathering
9. Simulated Live Teleseminars and Webinars
10. Email Broadcasting

Sign up at
www.MicroshareIntl.com/NewRules
for more information on how to use cross channel marketing to grow your business.

AUTOMATE YOUR FOLLOW-UP
CASE STUDY

An office cleaning company with a small sales force was struggling with consistently following up with prospects.

When we first met with the owner, Anthony, he complained that his staff seemed to be too late to get the sale. Too many times his team would follow up with prospects just days after they had already switched to a new cleaning company. It was a problem of time and timing. His salespeople just couldn't follow up enough to retain top of mind awareness. Because of this, many sales were lost.

We walked them through Rule 1 to 5, then created a follow-up sequence to automate their best sales presentations.

The first step was to gather all of their marketing material and make sure they had a clear concise message with a call to action.

Next, we videotaped the Anthony presenting their unique story, irresistible offer, and an overview of their services. Prospects could now experience the benefit of hearing and seeing their best presentation and getting to know, like and trust the company.

The sales people would meet prospects and enter the prospect's name and email into a web form right from their phone or company website and the prospect would be immediately in the sales funnel.

A couple times a month, the prospect would now receive high quality content from Anthony and team. His cleaning company was now front and center in the prospect's mind. When the prospect was ready to proceed, he had current information from the cleaning company and their contact information at his fingertips. (Top-of-mind awareness).

The Results

The funnel was filled, the sales people continued to do their best job, and the automated system did the rest. The new automated follow-up system funneled hot, prequalified, pre-sold customers from networking events, trade shows, and cold-calling efforts.

This synergistic relationship between sales people and automated tools increased sales significantly. Follow-up was no longer an issue and Anthony's frustrations were solved.

...Success!

www.MicroshareINTL.com/NewRules

RULE #7: TARGET NEW PROSPECTS

"[Marketing] is like playing the stock market, or being an atomic physicist.

All three deal with immense natural forces – gargantuan forces thousands of times more powerful than the men who use them.

In [marketing] they are the hopes and fears and desires of millions upon millions of men and woman all over the world."

- Eugene Schwartz

Companies have to continually find new, better and more efficient ways to market themselves. They must have a systematic approach that attracts Targeted Prospects and turns them into raving fans.

Targeting Top Prospects is essential to growing your business...

To succeed in the future you have to understand what Marketing tools are available and how to optimize them to target Top Prospects

Getting your business in front of more Targeted Prospects is easier than you would think.

Our world today is digital. Facebook boasts approximately 1 billion users, YouTube generates more than 4 billion video views daily, and there are more than 150 million blogs online.

There are more than 18 billion monthly searches conducted by U.S. internet users.

The Two Aspects of Lead Generation

When I consult with business owners, I tell them that there are two very distinct aspects of lead generations:

1. Hustle
2. Scientific Selling

Hustle is opportunistic. It is unique to your business, and a large part of successful hustle has to do with you—or your salespeople—being creative, charismatic and persuasive.

The two main focuses of hustle are dominating a community (a tribe) and developing power partnerships.

Hustle is a combination of grass roots marketing and traditional sales tactics.

If you, or your salespeople, are using this principle then you are…

- Going to strategic networking events
- Participating in trade shows

- Developing win-win relationships with other businesses
- Partnering with non-profits
- Delivering seminars and webinars to your target demographic
- Canvassing
- Cold Calling

The difficulty with hustle is that it is not formulaic, and your success will depend on your ability to think creatively and see unique opportunities.

Two great books that will help you with this process are:

- ***Getting Everything You Can Out of All You've Got***, by Jay Abraham
- ***No B.S. Grassroots Marketing***, by Dan Kennedy

A huge untapped opportunity for many businesses is in using the principles of hustle online.   This means using online tools to connect with people and develop relationships.

Try things like:

- Searching your 2nd level connections on LinkedIn and requesting an introduction
- Monitor Twitter for relevant conversation and join in
- Using your personal Facebook to stay connect to current clients and peers

This isn't for everyone, but it definitely works!

Scientific Selling

The second aspect of lead generation is much more analytical. The tactics used include:

- Direct Mail Marketing
- Acquisition Email Marketing
- Online Paid Advertising
- Media Buying

Most businesses start by applying the principles of Hustle: entrepreneurs work all hours to develop relationships, sell products, and create distribution channels.

I love working with businesses like this, applying the New Rules, and helping them increase their conversion rates significantly and pitch to power partners more successfully.

But at a certain point in a company's growth, it must become more methodical and analytical. And at this point marketing becomes much more strategic and analytical.

The great thing about scientific selling is that it is scalable. Once you develop a campaign that is successful, you will be able to increase its effectiveness by simply increasing your investment at a 1 to 1 ratio.

It is all about testing, tracking, and tweaking.

Ideal Client

Most successful scientific selling campaign are targeted towards a very specific audience.

For example, some companies generate 100% of their revenues by marketing to people who have already purchased a similar product. This was very common in old school direct mail information marketing companies. They would sell weight loss books to people who have already purchased weight loss books and business books to people who have already purchased business books.

There are hundreds, if not thousands of examples of companies who:

- Analyzed their current clients for trends
- Found that a large percentage of them had a certain characteristic (job, age, location, etc.)
- Focused their marketing on that demographic

- Reached significant growth

Mike Weinberg wrote a great article on, "The Who and Why Questions That Can Narrow the Field" that I highly recommend you reading.

If you want to expand your customer base, try narrowing your marketing message to focus on more specific customer needs rather than trying to convince everyone that you have the solution to their problems. Then you can focus on seven touches through cold calling, direct mail, email, customized post cards, and face-to-face meetings, etc.

Getting it Done

Targeting your best prospects can be completed in many ways, but there are really only three important factors:

1. Use methods that will target your best prospect, using the most effective strategy

2. Have a compelling message

3. Follow the other 6 Rules before you invest significant money in lead generation

Reminder: Targeting is the Last of the 7 New Rules!

I want to repeat myself to make sure you understand that these Rules are a systematic framework, and you must address Rules 1-6 before you try to Target Top Prospects—especially with scientific selling.

Do you:

- Have an effective strategy?

- Control the conversation with prospects?
- Dominate your industry online?
- Command authority?
- Market your outstanding reputation?
- Automate follow-up effectively?

www.MicroshareINTL.com/NewRules

Target your Top Prospects with:

1. Sales People
2. JV's and Power Partners
3. Acquisition Email Marketing
4. Direct Mail
5. PPC (Pay Per Click Ads)

Sign up at
www.MicroshareIntl.com/NewRules
for a video that will teach you more
about tools for
Targeting Top Prospects

LAST CASE STUDY: MICROSHARE INTL

We entered the marketing arena offering an effective and cutting edge online marketing solution.

Combining this X-factor with Barry's numerous business successes, we had a convincing company story.

We also put together a decent website. Just with these two components our business started to grow.

Next, we developed our Local Online Presence and hosted free and paid seminars and webinars. We began developing momentum.

Then, we shot video testimonials and used them to close our biggest deal yet.

We automated our sales and noticed a much more consistent stream of qualified leads which led to increased sales. This was our first cycle through the framework...

Then, we started all over.

www.MicroshareINTL.com/NewRules

We worked on better offers and started focusing our efforts towards a more narrow audience (this made a huge difference). We redesigned our web-site, sought out and attained Board of Director and Chairman positions at quality organizations as well as systematized and automated our Reputation Marketing. (Repeated Rules a second time)

And, again, a third time.

We wrote and published a book (the one you're reading now), we updated our website again, we began a direct mail campaign...

Here is the important part:

- We went through the Rules the first time and we were marginally successful. Most of our business came from networking and warm leads.
- We went through the rules a second time; we grew our business, and our conversions and referrals increased.

- We went through the framework a third time and our business became consistent. Consistent leads, consistent high monthly earning, and consistently satisfied customers.

The Results

Each time, there was success. We advanced our knowledge and authority as well as increased our efficiency and revenue.

The key is realizing that business and the world don't stop changing; you, your marketing efforts and your business must also continually be focused on growth and improving to the next level.

It is simply going upward one step at a time.

Success!

www.MicroshareINTL.com/NewRules

CONCLUSION

Congratulations! By finishing this book you have completed a 7 Step Marketing Course. If you are a current marketer, you now know more about marketing in the New World than 90% of your peers, and if you are a business owner, you probably know more than 99% of your competition.

It is time to first celebrate your victory. Several hours ago, or several days ago you created a goal of finishing this book, and now you have accomplished this goal. As I teach in my book *Success Junkie*, it is very important to take time, even if it can only be a brief moment, to celebrate this victory. Recognize that you are one step closer to reaching your Vision and be joyous. Know that I am proud of your success and very grateful that you took the time to listen to my teachings.

Your next step is to use these Rules to create a written plan, and then take indomitable action!

ABOUT THE AUTHORS

Barry Schimmel has been an entrepreneur for over 20 years and has founded three multi-million dollar companies.

His client experience is deep and includes Pepsi Cola Bottling Co., American Express, and Temple Inland, among many others.

- Barry earned his MBA in Marketing for Roosevelt University and is a veteran of the United States Army.
- He is a member of America's Premier Experts, and the Experts Industry Association.
- He sits on the Board of Directors for the Barrington Area Chamber of Commerce.
- His TV interview with Brian Tracy will soon appear on ABC, CBS, NBC and Fox.

www.MicroshareINTL.com/NewRules

In 2010, Barry began teaching what he describes as "the lessons learned through the millions of mistakes along the way." He has inspired thousands across the United States.

To your outrageous success!

www.MicroshareINTL.com/NewRules

Grant Polachek started his entrepreneurial journey at 15 years old, when he grew the second largest satellite karate program for the largest martial arts organization in the Mid-West.

He later became a member of their Board of Directors, and helped grow four consecutive karate programs to their highest monthly gross.

- Grant is the Chair of the Barrington Area Chamber of Commerce's Marketing Council.
- He is Google Engage Partner, Inbound Marketing Certified, and Cross Channel Marketing Certified.

7 New Marketing Rules reached the Amazon Best Sellers list, the Amazon Hot New Releases List, and the Amazon Top Rated List.

OTHER BOOKS BY BARRY AND GRANT

Success Junkie: 12 Principles for Winning the Life of your Dreams

A Message to Entrepreneurs and Executives: 7 Lenses for Overcoming Stagnation and Troubleshooting your Agonizing Business Problems

www.MicroshareINTL.com/NewRules

GRANT AND BARRY CURRENTLY SPEAK ON...

- The 7 New Marketing Rules
- The Power of Upsells, Downsells and Cross Sells: Grow your business 50%, 100%, 200% or even 2000%
- Modern Marketing Strategy
- Modern Marketing for Authors, Experts, Speakers and Consultants
- Making Money With Your Website
- Domination your Competition with Local Online Marketing
- Building Authority in a New Age
- Reputation Marketing
- Marketing Automation
- Lead Generation

www.MicroshareINTL.com/NewRules

www.MicroshareINTL.com/NewRules

"Barry and Grant may as well have invented marketing in the technological age. My list growth was beyond stagnant for well over a year. Then I had my home page redesigned according to their system and I now experience a rate of daily opt ins that is exceeding my expectations. It's an exciting change."

- Brian R. King,
  www.BrianRaymondKing.com

"I picked up new ideas everyone should have, no matter how big or small their company."

- Hazel Wagner, www.HazelWagner.com
  Former instructor, Kellogg Graduate School of Management

"The information in Barry & Grant's new book is short, concise... to the point! Get it - read it - get going!

- Jared Silver, Founder At a Glance Marketing.

"I found this to be a great book for clear and practical steps on how to market my business on-line and off-line! The 7 New Marketing Rules clearly shows the latest tools and resources to create a step-by-step marketing strategy that gets results. What I liked best is that The 7 New Marketing Rules "gets" how important reputation is and shows me how simple it is to use positive feedback and comments from my clients to attract more business. I recommend this book to anyone."

- Laurie Polinski, www.BreakthroughCoachingAdvantage.com

"Barry & Grant deliver the goods. They don't just preach and teach strategy, they implement it - for themselves and their clients. Their proven system is truly proven day in and day out with the results they get. And that's what it's all about. Use this book to launch your business or take it to the next level. Grow your business quickly and easily with their 7 New Marketing Rules.

- Kelly Epperson, www.BirthThatBook.com

"Barry and Grant continue to give and give. The step by step guide gives you all you need to move your marketing forward. Novice or expert - you will learn from this straight forward process. The best part - it works!"

- Andrea Herran, www.FocusHR.biz

"Barry and Grant have produced a gem in this book...a simple, down-to-earth, duplicatable process to market your business now. Employing their 7 New

Marketing Rules not only helped us build loyalty among our tribe, but it has helped us further a reputation of integrity with prospective clients. In a world that is inundated with marketing messages, this book cuts to the chase and helps you do the most effective things first without wasting lots of time and money on wild marketing goose chases."

- Gail Brown,
  www.EngagingSpeakers.com

"I'm already seeing results and I'm only half-way through the book."

- Mark Papadas,
  www.IAm4KidsFoundation.org

"7 New Marketing Rules is one of the most informative marketing publications I have read. Barry and Grant provide real substantive information about MicroShare INTL's proven results based marketing techniques… This powerful marketing system is even more illuminating when you introduce the benefit of their actual Case Studies. I would recommend it as an excellent addition to your professional library."

- Eric Zitron, President of Z-Marketing

"Barry and Grant's 7 New Marketing Rules provides tools that deliver immediate results. Easy to implement and cost effective, these rules ARE growing my business. I wish I had it 5 years ago."

- Mike Imm, Barrington Allstate Agent

NOTES

NOTES

NOTES

NOTES

NOTES

www.MicroshareINTL.com/NewRules

NOTES

NOTES

www.MicroshareINTL.com/NewRules

NOTES

www.MicroshareINTL.com/NewRules

Cover art by
Grant Polachek

www.MicroshareINTL.com/NewRules

www.ingramcontent.com/pod-product-compliance
Lightning Source LLC
Chambersburg PA
CBHW051705170526
45167CB00002B/548